For my granddaughters
Lyla, Noa & Orli

I love you to the moon and back

Calling all story explorers!
Join our mailing list for
discount offers
,monthly newsletter
& new releases
Be the first to know of every new tale.

timeless Stories By Yaffa turgeman

https://amazon.com/author/yaffaturgeman
www.yaffaturgeman.com

50 Tips To Improve Your Child's Listening Skills

Paperback

ISBN- 979-8271142741

Printed in united States

Disclaimer-Yaffa Turgeman is
A Registered Trademark

🎧 **Guess what? Stories can travel with you!**
Listen in the car 🚗
Listen during quiet time 🌳
Listen before bedtime 🌙
👨‍👩‍👧 Parents:
Visit my author page to check each book's format and
find stories available as audiobooks for
listening anytime.
📖 ✨ https://amazon.com/author/yaffaturgeman
🎶 It's story time... wherever you are!
Sit back, relax,
use your listening ears,
and let the story take you on an adventure ✨

1- Dedication

Content - 2-5

6- **Building foundation**

7- Tip #1 Model good listening by giving your child your full attention.

8- Tip #2 Use daily routines to practice listening.

9- Tip #3 Say your   child's name first before giving directions

10- Tip #4 Use a gentle touch on the shoulder to gain attention.

11- Tip #5 Keep instructions short and clear

12- Tip #6 Give one step at a time, especially for younger kids.

13- Tip#7 Allow a pause for your child to process before repeating.

14- Tip -Tip #8 Speak calmly and slowly instead of rushing.

15- Tip #9 Use daily routines so children know what to expect.

16- Tip #10 Avoid calling out from another room.

17- **Creating a Listening environment**

18- Tip #11 Turn off background noise before speaking.

19- Tip #12 Reduce clutter and noise to help focus.

20- Tip #13 Sit in a quiet, well-lit space for important talks.

21- Tip #14 Keep listening times short and age-appropriate.

22- Tip #15 Give advance notice: "In two minutes, I need you to listen."

23- **Communication techniques**

24- Tip #16 Start with positive words: "I need your help with…"

25- Tip #17 Ask your child to repeat back what they heard

26- Tip # 18 Use visual cues — charts, pictures, or gestures content

27- Tip # 19   Clap or ring a bell as a listening signal.

28- Tip #20 Break tasks into "first, then" steps.

29- **Encouragements and praises.**

30- **Mistakes are part of the learning curve.**

31- Tip #21 Notice and praise good listening right away.

32- Tip #22 Use specific praise.

33- Tip #23 Give small rewards for listening milestones.

34- Tip # 24 Celebrate with a high five or hug when they listen well.

35- Tip #25 Encourage effort, not perfection.

36- **Fun Practice at home.**

37- **Make listening playful.**

38- Tip # 26 Encourage effort, not perfection.

39- Tip #27 Play Telephone to sharpen memory and focus.

40- **Show closeness while listening.**
41- Tip # 28 Read aloud and ask prediction questions.
42- Tip #29 Sing songs together that require echo responses.
43- Tip # 30 Use silly listening games.
44- **Every day listening habits.**
45- Tip # 31 Give directions during natural routines (meal time, bedtime).
46- Tip #32 Involve children in chores with step-by-step tasks.
47- Tip# 33 Ask questions during car rides to practice focus.

48- Tip # 34 Turn errands into listening games: "Find the item I just named.
49-Tip #35 Share family stories that require attention and recall.
50- **Emotional connection**
51- Tip# 36 Offer physical closeness — sit side by side while talking.
52- Tip# 37 Make eye contact and smile often.
53-Tip# 38 Use gentle humor to keep attention light.
54-Tip# 39 Avoid scolding while giving instructions; stay calm.
55-Tip# 40 Listen to them first — model respect by hearing their thoughts.

A Letter to Parents

If there is one thing I hope you take with you from this book, it is this:
Listening is not about obedience.
It is about connection.
Children don't learn to listen because they are told to.
They learn to listen because they feel heard, understood, and safe.

Listening grows in everyday moments — not when everything is calm and perfect, but in the middle of busy mornings, emotional afternoons, and tired evenings. It grows when we pause, soften our tone, and choose connection over control.

The tips in this book are not theoretical ideas. They are based on over 30 years of hands-on experience working with children and families, as the owner and educational director of my own early childhood center. Over the years, I have listened to thousands of children — and just as importantly, to their parents. I have seen what helps children open their ears and hearts, and what makes them shut down.

And what I've learned is this:
Children listen best when they feel respected.
They cooperate more when they feel understood.
And they grow when listening becomes a shared experience — not a power struggle.

Some days, listening will come easily.
Other days, it will feel frustrating, exhausting, or out of reach.
That doesn't mean you're doing anything wrong.
You do not need to use all 50 tips at once. You don't need to remember them all. Choose one or two that speak to you. Try them gently. Return to this book when you need support, ideas, or reassurance.
Your presence matters more than perfect words.
Your calm matters more than control.
Your willingness to listen matters more than getting it right every time.
And just as your child needs to learn how to listen —
you deserve to feel listened to as well.
You are learning.
You are growing.
And every small moment of connection makes a difference.
Because when children feel heard,
they learn to listen.
With care and belief in you,
Yaffa Turgeman

Model good listening by giving your child your full attention. #1

When you pause what you're doing, make eye contact, and truly listen, your child feels valued and understood. This simple act teaches them that listening matters — and helps them learn to give the same respect in return.

Use daily routines to practice listening. #2

Everyday moments like mealtime, bedtime, or getting dressed are great chances to practice listening. Simple directions such as "Put your spoon on the plate" or "Brush your teeth before bed" help children focus without pressure.

When listening becomes part of daily life, it feels natural and positive. This builds focus, cooperation, and confidence as children learn to anticipate what comes next and take responsibility.

Say your child's name first before giving directions. #3

Start by saying your child's name to gently signal, "I need your attention." It helps them pause what they're doing and focus on you.

This small step makes your message clear and personal, reducing distractions and improving communication. Over time, it strengthens attention, understanding, and connection.

Use a gentle touch on the shoulder to gain attention. #4

A light touch on the shoulder or arm is a warm, respectful way to say, "I'm here—please listen." It feels kinder and calmer than calling out from across the room. This small gesture helps your child pause, refocus, and feel safe. Over time, it builds trust and teaches that listening moments can be calm and connected, not stressful.

Keep instructions short and clear. #5

Children understand and remember better when directions are simple. Long or complicated instructions can confuse them. Give one clear step at a time—like "Please put your shoes by the door." This helps them stay focused, succeed quickly, and build confidence. Over time, short, clear guidance strengthens listening, focus, and independence.

Give one step at a time, especially for younger kids. #6

Young children can get overwhelmed by too many directions at once. Breaking tasks into small, clear steps helps them focus and succeed.

For example, say, "First pick up the blocks," then, "Put the books on the shelf." Step-by-step guidance builds confidence, problem-solving skills, and the habit of listening carefully.

Allow a pause for your child to process before repeating.
#7

Children often need a few extra seconds to think and respond. Jumping in too quickly or repeating yourself can overwhelm them.
A short pause after giving directions shows patience and respect for their pace. It helps them feel capable, think independently, and respond more thoughtfully.

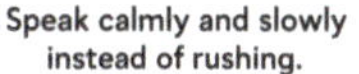

Speak calmly and slowly instead of rushing. #8

Children listen best when your voice is calm and steady. A gentle tone helps them feel safe and focused, while rushed or sharp words can cause stress or shut down listening.

Speaking slowly gives children time to process and follow directions. It also models patience and self-control—showing them how calm communication builds respect and cooperation.

Use consistent daily routines
so children know what to expect.

Use daily routines so children know what to expect. #9

Children feel calm and confident when life is predictable. Simple routines—like morning steps, mealtime, or bedtime—create structure they can trust.

When kids know what comes next, there's less resistance and more cooperation. Routines also build memory, responsibility, and focus by giving children a steady rhythm they can rely on.

Avoid calling out from another room. #10

Shouting from across the house rarely works — children may be too busy or unsure if you're speaking to them. Walk over, kneel, and speak face-to-face. This shows respect, helps your child see your expression, and builds trust and focus. Over time, it teaches true listening and strengthens your connection.

🎧 Creating a
Listening Environment

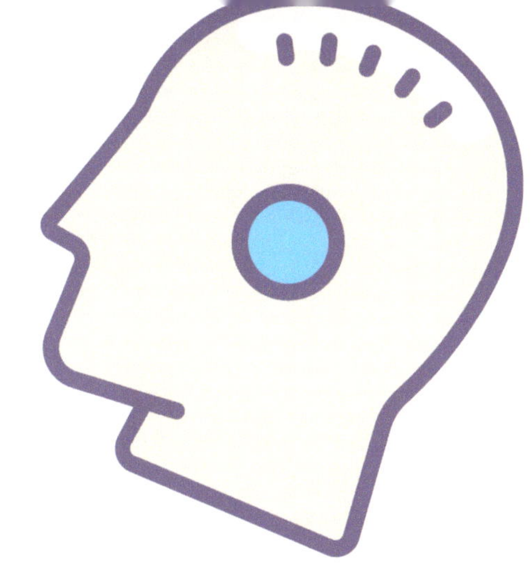

Turn off background noise before speaking. #11

Children can't easily tune out distractions like TV, music, or chatter. A calm, quiet space helps them focus fully on your words. Turning off background noise shows that what you're saying is important and teaches respect for listening. Over time, this builds focus, understanding, and good communication habits.

Reduce clutter and noise to help focus. #12

Children find it hard to tune out
background sounds like TV or music.
Turning off distractions before speaking
helps them focus fully on you.
A quiet environment sends the message that
your words matter. Over time, this teaches
respect and shows that listening means
giving full attention.

Sit in a quiet, well-lit space for important talks #13

Children focus better in calm, clutter-free spaces. Too many toys or distractions make it hard for them to listen and follow directions.

A tidy, well-lit environment helps their brain relax and signals it's time to pay attention. Keeping the area organized doesn't remove fun — it simply makes listening and learning easier.

Keep listening times short and age-appropriate. #14

Children listen best in calm, focused environments. Turn off distractions, reduce noise, and keep the space bright and comfortable.

A peaceful setting helps them feel safe, focused, and open to hearing you. Over time, they'll associate quiet, clear moments with positive communication and easier listening.

Give advance notice: "In two minutes, I need you to listen."
#15

Children focus best when they know what's coming. Letting them know a few minutes ahead helps them shift attention calmly instead of feeling rushed.
Keep instructions short and age-appropriate—break long talks into quick, clear moments. When children succeed at listening in small steps, it builds confidence, focus, and a positive habit of paying attention.

Communication Techniques

Start with positive words: "I need your help with…" #16

Positive language turns pressure into cooperation. Saying "I know you can do this" instead of "You never listen" builds trust and confidence.

When children feel respected and capable, they listen more willingly. Over time, positive words teach them to use kindness in their own communication—strengthening confidence, connection, and motivation to help.

Ask your child to repeat back what they heard #17

When children repeat instructions in their own words, it shows they understood—and gives a chance to fix confusion right away.

This simple habit strengthens memory, focus, and communication. For example, after saying, "Please put your homework in your backpack," follow with, "Can you tell me what you'll do next?"

Repeating turns listening into an active skill and builds lifelong responsibility and confidence.

Use visual cues — charts, pictures, or gestures #18

Children often need more than words to understand directions. Visual cues—like charts, pictures, or simple gestures—make instructions clearer and easier to remember.

A morning routine chart or a parent pointing to their ear while saying "Listen carefully" helps reinforce messages without repeating. Visuals also boost confidence, focus, and independence, turning listening into a skill children can manage on their own.

Clap or ring a bell as a listening signal #19

A gentle sound—like a clap, chime, or small bell—tells children it's time to pause and listen without raising your voice. Over time, they learn to associate the sound with focus and calm attention.

This simple cue reduces frustration, cuts through distractions, and helps create a peaceful, respectful listening environment at home or in class.

Break tasks into "first, then" steps #20

Too many instructions can overwhelm children. Breaking tasks into small steps—like "First put on your shoes, then we'll go outside"—helps them focus and succeed one step at a time.

This approach reduces stress, builds confidence, and teaches sequencing and patience. Step-by-step progress makes even big tasks feel doable.

Encouragement & Praise

Mistakes as a learning curve

Children learn and grow through practice, and mistakes are a natural part of that journey. If parents focus only on perfection, children may feel anxious, discouraged, or afraid to try new things. But when parents notice and praise the effort—whether the result is "perfect" or not—they send the message that trying, learning, and improving matter most.

For example, saying, "I love how hard you worked to listen and follow my directions," even if the child missed a step, teaches them that persistence is valued. This kind of feedback builds confidence, because children realize they don't have to be flawless to be appreciated. It also fosters resilience, showing them that mistakes are simply part of learning, not reasons to give up. When effort is celebrated, children are more motivated to keep practicing and growing. They learn that progress comes step by step, and that every attempt is a success in its own way. Over time, this approach shapes a healthy mindset where listening, learning, and life itself are about growth—
not perfection.

Notice and praise good listening right away #21

Children stay motivated when their efforts are noticed. Simple praise like, "I love how carefully you listened just now," helps them connect listening with pride and success. Immediate encouragement builds confidence and strengthens the parent-child bond, showing kids that effort matters just as much as results.

Use specific praise:
"I love how you looked at me when I spoke." #22

Praise right after good listening helps children connect their actions to positive feelings. Be specific—"Thank you for listening right away!"—so they know exactly what they did well.

Immediate, clear praise boosts confidence and encourages them to keep listening because they feel noticed and appreciated.

Give small rewards for listening milestones #23

Immediate praise helps children connect their effort to success. When you say, "Great job listening the first time!" or offer a sticker or extra playtime, they understand what behavior to repeat.

Quick, positive feedback builds confidence and motivation. Over time, listening becomes a source of pride—not just for the reward, but for the feeling of doing something well.

Celebrate with a high five or hug when they listen well #24

Children love recognition. Simple rewards—like stickers, extra playtime, or a big smile—show that effort matters. These moments make listening feel fun and meaningful. Small celebrations help children stay motivated and proud of their progress. Over time, they learn that the real reward isn't the sticker—it's the confidence and joy that come from listening well.

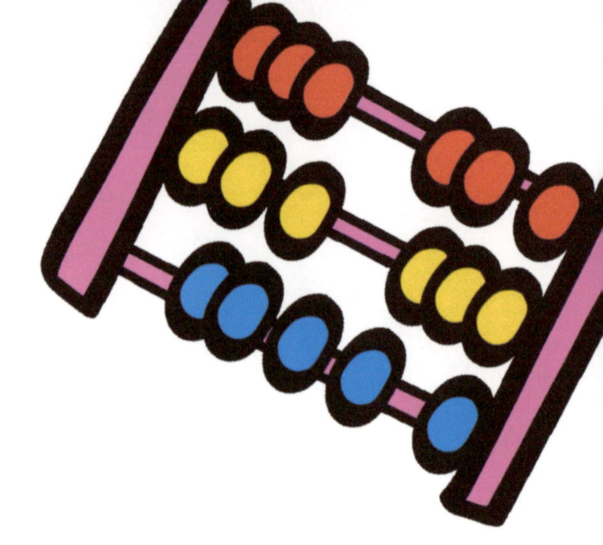

Encourage effort, not perfection #25

Celebrate your child's effort right away—a smile, high five, or hug says, "I see you and I'm proud of you." These small moments make a big impact, connecting effort with love and joy.

Simple, warm praise motivates children to keep listening, not for rewards, but for the pride and connection it brings. Over time, this builds confidence and creates a lasting habit of positive listening.

Fun Practice at Home

Make listening playful

Children learn best through fun!
Turning listening into games, songs, or
playful challenges keeps them focused
and eager to join in.
When listening feels like play—through
"Simon Says" or silly challenges—kids
relax, enjoy learning, and build
confidence. A playful attitude turns
everyday moments into lasting
listening habits.

Encourage effort, not perfection
#26

The game Simon Says helps children build focus, patience, and self-control. To play, kids must listen closely and act only when they hear "Simon says," which trains them to think before reacting.

This playful activity turns listening into fun practice. It strengthens attention, memory, and the ability to follow directions—essential skills for school and life.

Play Telephone to sharpen memory and focus #27

The classic game Telephone makes listening fun while teaching focus and memory. Each child must listen carefully, remember the message, and repeat it clearly—learning how easily words can change when attention slips.

This lighthearted game builds concentration, patience, and communication skills. Whether using short phrases or silly sentences, it turns listening practice into laughter and teamwork.

Read aloud and ask prediction questions #28

When reading together, pause and ask your child what they think will happen next. This simple question turns listening into active thinking and sparks imagination.
Children learn to connect story clues, follow the sequence of events, and strengthen memory and focus. Predicting also boosts confidence—showing them that their ideas matter and that listening closely helps them understand and enjoy stories more deeply.

Sing songs together that require echo responses #29

Echo songs turn listening into a fun, musical game. As children repeat each line, they practice focus, rhythm, and clear speech. The repetition builds memory, confidence, and language skills—while the shared singing time strengthens connection between child and adult. Listening becomes joyful, social, and full of music and laughter.

Use silly listening games #30

Make listening fun with playful activities like "Hop when you hear the word cat!" Games like these turn focus practice into excitement.

Children learn to pay attention, remember instructions, and respond at the right time—all while moving and laughing. When listening feels like play, kids stay engaged, confident, and eager to keep practicing every day.

🏡Everyday Listening Habits

Give directions during natural routines (mealtime, bedtime) #31

Listening becomes stronger through daily habits. Using natural moments—like mealtime, bedtime, or play—to give directions helps children practice focus, cooperation, and empathy.

When listening is part of everyday life, kids learn to follow instructions, respect others, and connect more deeply with family and friends. Over time, this simple routine builds both confidence and caring communication.

Involve children in chores with step-by-step tasks #32

Chores teach more than tidiness—they build
listening, focus, and responsibility.
Breaking tasks into small, clear steps ("Wipe
the table, then put the dishes away") helps
children follow directions, stay organized, and
feel confident completing each part.
Over time, they learn that careful listening
and teamwork make even big jobs easy—and
success comes one step at a time.

Ask questions during car rides to practice focus #33

Car rides are perfect for building listening and thinking skills. With fewer distractions, children can truly focus on conversation.

Ask simple questions like, "What do you see out the window?" or "What do you think we'll have for dinner?" to spark curiosity and reflection.

These talks strengthen attention, memory, and imagination while deepening your bond—turning everyday drives into moments of connection and growth.

Turn errands into listening games: "Find the item I just named." #34

Everyday errands can become fun learning moments. Asking, "Can you find the apples?" helps children practice listening, remembering, and following directions.

These small tasks build focus, responsibility, and confidence while turning routine errands into playful teamwork.

Listening becomes part of real life—fun, interactive, and full of cooperation.

Share family stories that require attention and recall #35

Children love hearing stories from their own family—they listen closely and want to remember every detail.

Family storytelling builds memory, focus, and listening skills while creating a sense of belonging. It teaches where they come from, highlights family values, and keeps traditions alive.

When you share memories like "When I was your age," listening becomes more than learning—it becomes connection, love, and legacy.

❤️Emotional Connection

Offer physical closeness – sit side by side while talking #36

Children listen best when they feel safe, loved, and understood. Sitting close and showing gentle attention helps them feel accepted and valued.

When children know their feelings matter, they open up more easily and listen in return. This closeness builds trust, empathy, and confidence—turning listening into a shared act of care and connection.

Make eye contact and smile often
#37

Looking into your child's eyes says, "I see you, and I'm listening." It builds trust and shows full attention.

A warm smile adds comfort and reassurance, helping your child feel safe and valued.

Together, eye contact and smiling create connection and respect—turning listening into a moment of love and understanding, not instruction.

Use gentle humor to keep attention light #38

Humor builds connection and makes listening fun. A playful tone, funny voice, or silly exaggeration helps children relax and stay engaged.

Gentle humor turns pressure into joy—saying something like, "Quick, the socks are running away!" invites cooperation instead of resistance.

Shared laughter strengthens trust and makes learning feel enjoyable, showing that listening can be filled with joy, not stress.

Avoid scolding while giving instructions; stay calm #39

How directions are spoken matters. A calm, kind tone helps children feel safe and open to listening.

Scolding or yelling can cause fear and defensiveness, making it harder for kids to focus or cooperate.

Using a gentle voice models self-control and respect. It shows children that communication can be calm and caring, even during correction—building trust and healthy emotional habits over time.

Listen to them first — model respect by hearing their thoughts
#40

When parents listen before correcting, they show children that their voice matters. This builds respect, trust, and cooperation.
Hearing your child's perspective turns potential conflict into connection. It also teaches that good communication is a two-way exchange — listening is just as important as speaking.
By modeling this respect, you strengthen your bond and teach empathy, patience, and understanding.

Consistency & Patience

Building strong listening skills takes time and patience

Listening grows through repetition, clear expectations, and gentle guidance. When parents stay consistent, children feel secure and understand what's expected. Mistakes and distractions are part of learning. Calm patience teaches kids that growth takes practice, not perfection. Over time, steady consistency and encouragement build confidence, resilience, and trust—creating a positive environment where children can truly thrive.

Repeat instructions patiently, without anger #41

When children don't follow directions right away, they may be distracted or still processing. Calmly repeating instructions gives them a chance to understand without feeling pressured.

Patience shows, "I believe in you," helping kids feel safe and supported. Anger, on the other hand, can create stress and make it harder for them to listen.

Responding with calm repetition builds trust, self-control, and resilience—teaching that listening improves through patience, not pressure.

Set clear, consistent rules about listening at home #42

Children thrive on clarity and routine. When rules stay the same, kids know what's expected—reducing confusion and frustration.
Simple guidelines like "Look at the speaker" or "Wait your turn to talk" help children practice respectful listening. Consistency teaches them that listening matters in every situation.
Clear rules build trust, respect, and self-control—turning listening into a natural part of family life.

Build listening into daily routines: "Story, then bedtime." #43

When listening becomes part of everyday routines, it turns into a natural habit. A bedtime story is a simple way to build calm, connection, and consistency.

Repeating the same routine helps children know what to expect and makes transitions smoother.

They learn that listening isn't a chore—it's part of love, comfort, and family time.

These small daily moments strengthen both attention and your bond together.

Use countdowns ("In seconds, it's time to listen") #44

Transitions can be tough for kids. Countdowns help by giving a gentle warning before change happens.

Saying things like, "In five minutes we'll clean up," or "When I count to three, it's time to listen," allows children to finish what they're doing and prepare to switch tasks calmly. This simple habit builds patience, time awareness, and cooperation—turning transitions into smoother, stress-free moments.

Be patient — listening is a skill that grows with time #45

Listening develops gradually, just like learning to ride a bike. Children need time and practice to build focus, memory, and self-control.

Each time you remind your child to stop, pay attention, or follow directions, you're helping them strengthen this skill.

Be patient and consistent. With encouragement and practice, children learn that mistakes are part of growth—and their listening confidence will steadily bloom.

Expanding Skills

Expanding skills helps children grow in every direction

Children thrive when they explore different areas of learning—reading, music, art, gardening, cooking, or sports. Each activity strengthens creativity, teamwork, and confidence.

Through hands-on experiences, kids learn problem-solving, communication, and self-expression. They discover their strengths and how to connect with others.

Expanding skills prepares children for life by building resilience, adaptability, and the confidence to face challenges with a positive spirit.

Encourage listening to grandparents, teachers, and siblings #46

Children learn valuable lessons not only from parents but also through listening to grandparents, teachers, and siblings. Each relationship teaches something unique.

Listening to grandparents connects children to family stories, values, and traditions—building identity and respect.

Teachers model structure and guidance, helping kids follow instructions and work with others.

Siblings teach cooperation, empathy, and patience through daily interactions.

When children listen in these relationships, they strengthen respect, understanding, and family bonds that last a lifetime.

Attend library story times for extra listening practice #47

Library story times are more than fun—they help children become better listeners. Focusing on the reader's voice and story builds attention, comprehension, and imagination.
Hearing different readers exposes kids to new tones and styles, teaching them to listen carefully and patiently in a group setting.
Most of all, story times show that listening opens the door to new ideas, friendships, and adventures—making learning joyful and lasting.

Play audiobooks or podcasts made for kids #48

Audiobooks and children's podcasts turn listening into a fun adventure. They help kids focus on voices, words, and tone—strengthening attention, imagination, and comprehension. As children listen, they picture characters and stories in their minds, building creativity and curiosity. They also learn new vocabulary, rhythm, and the beauty of storytelling. Listening this way shows kids that learning can be exciting, inspiring a lifelong love for stories and discovery.

Give opportunities to share what they heard at school #49

When children retell what they learned at school, they strengthen memory, understanding, and confidence. Explaining in their own words helps them recall details and make real connections — showing they truly listened. When parents listen with interest, children feel proud that their voice matters. These conversations build trust, communication skills, and lasting family connection.

Teach empathy — remind them that listening shows love and care. #50

Empathy begins with listening — noticing words, tone, and body language. When children truly listen, they understand how others feel and respond with kindness.

Practicing empathy can be simple: sharing a toy, giving a hug, or saying kind words. These small actions help children build strong friendships and caring hearts.

Listening with empathy turns attention into love — a lifelong skill that nurtures compassion and connection.

Make listening fun, creative, and lasting - one coloring page at a time!

Pair it with "50 Tips to Improve Your Child's Listening Skills- coloring book" for the full learning experience.

- **Why Parents Love It:**

- Reinforces positive listening habits in a fun, hands-on way
- Builds focus, patience, and empathy through art
- Encourages parent-child connection and meaningful conversations

https://www.amazon.com/author/yaffaturgeman

Perfect for home, classrooms, or therapy settings Whether your child is coloring a scene about taking turns, focusing on instructions, or showing care through listening - this book helps transform important life lessons into joyful moments.

We'd love your help!
please take a moment to leave
a review on Amazon.
Your feedback not only means the
world to us, but it also helps other
parents discover this book and bring
Joyful moments
into their homes.

Thank you for your support
https://amazon.com/author/yaffaturgeman
For other books by author Yaffa turgeman
visit us-
www.yaffaturgeman.com

Follow us on:
TikTok- Yaffa Turgeman
Facebook- Yaffa Turgeman
Instagram- Yaffa Turgeman
FB page- Timeless Stories By Yaffa Turgeman

Yaffa Turgeman dedicated over thirty years to working with children, as the owner and educational director of her preschool. With love and devotion, she nurtured children of all ages and responded to their needs with sensitivity and care.

Now retired, Yaffa has chosen to devote her time to two lifelong passions: writing children's literature and creating cookbooks.

In each of her books, she weaves together her love for childhood, imagination, flavors, and traditions—preserving cherished memories and passing on stories and recipes filled with warmth, color, and soul for generations to come

www.yaffaturgeman.com